AF228938

IMMIGRANT CONTRIBUTIONS

Cornerstone of American Prosperity

Barbara Sheen

ReferencePoint Press

San Diego, CA

Picture Credits:

Cover: Atelier211/Shutterstock (top left); BearFotos/Shutterstock (top right); Prostock-studio/Shutterstock (middle); Wazzkii/Shutterstock (bottom left); Odua Images/Shutterstock (bottom right)

4: Shutterstock
5: Shutterstock
8: ZUMA Press, Inc./Alamy Stock Photo
12: Peter Newark American Pictures/Bridgeman Images
15: StockImageFactory.com/Shutterstock

20: Martin Klimek/ZUMAPRESS/Newscom
24: Associated Press
28: Sean Pavone/Shutterstock
30: Associated Press
35: Stuart Monk/Shutterstock
37: David Litschel/Alamy Stock Photo
41: Cal Sport Media/Alamy Stock Photo
46: Peter DaSilva/Polaris/Newscom
50: Associated Press
55: Associated Press

Charts and graphs by Maury Aaseng

LIBRARY OF CONGRESS CATALOGING-IN-PUBLICATION DATA

Names: Sheen, Barbara, author.
Title: Immigrant contributions : cornerstone of American prosperity / by Barbara Sheen.
Description: San Diego, CA : ReferencePoint Press, 2025. | Includes bibliographical references and index.
Identifiers: LCCN 2024004103 (print) | LCCN 2024004104 (ebook) | ISBN 9781678208042 (library binding) | ISBN 9781678208059 (ebook)
Subjects: LCSH: Immigrants--United States--Juvenile literature. | United States--Emigration and immigration--Juvenile literature.
Classification: LCC E184.A1 S573 2025 (print) | LCC E184.A1 (ebook) | DDC 305.800973--dc23/eng/20240304
LC record available at https://lccn.loc.gov/2024004103
LC ebook record available at https://lccn.loc.gov/2024004104

CONTENTS

IMMIGRANT CONTRIBUTIONS TO AMERICAN PROSPERITY

US Immigrant Population

46.2 million, or 13.9% of total US population, in 2022

Top Six Countries of Origin

Mexico: 24%   India: 6%   China: 5%
Philippines: 5%   El Salvador: 3%   Vietnam: 3%

Earnings of Immigrant Workers

Immigrant

| Low Wage 35% | Middle Wage 48% | Upper Wage 17% |

65% of Immigrant Workers Earn Middle Wages or Higher

US Born

| Low Wage 26% | Middle Wage 57% | Upper Wage 17% |

74% of US-Born Workers Earn Middle Wages or Higher

Fortune 500 Companies

As of 2023, 44.8% were founded by immigrants or their children

Immigrants in the Workforce

(as of Sept. 2023)
30.21 million, or 19% of US workers

Immigrant Occupations

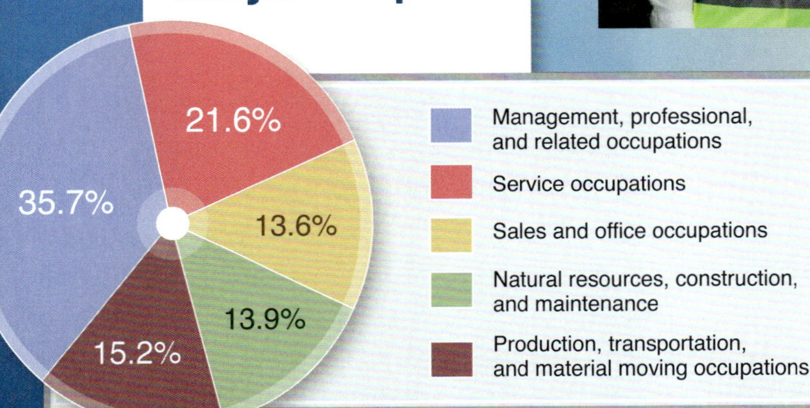

Immigrant Entrepreneurs

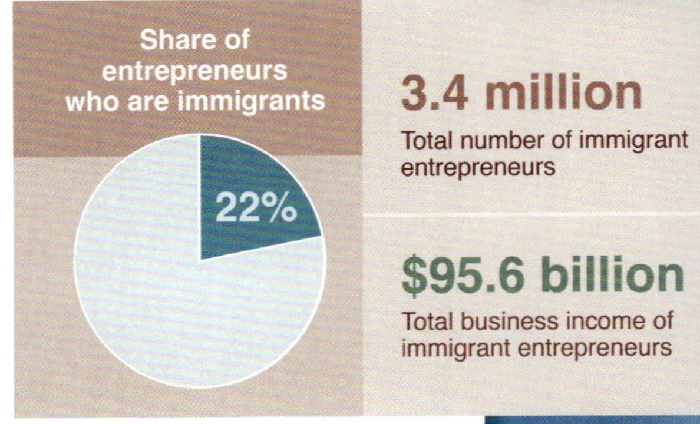

Taxes and Spending

$1.9 trillion
Immigrant household income

$1.4 trillion
Total spending power

$524.7 billion
Total taxes paid

Immigrants Help Drive American Prosperity

Mario Tommolillo is an Italian American whose family immigrated to the United States in 1967 in pursuit of a better life. He was eleven years old at the time. "We were so excited to become part of the best country in the world,"[1] he recalls.

The family settled in New Jersey, where Tommolillo attended school and worked in a hardware store in the evening. After graduating from high school, he accepted a job at an auto dealership, where he worked for the next two decades. During this time, he married, raised two daughters, and became a naturalized US citizen (a foreign-born person who becomes a US citizen). During the 1990s, he bought an auto body shop in Paterson, New Jersey. Under his leadership, the shop grew from a very small business to a firm that earns over $2 million a year and employs fourteen people.

Over the years, Tommolillo has become a respected figure in Paterson. He serves on the boards of several organizations that support local causes. Like millions of other immigrants, Tommolillo embraced the opportunities that life in the United States has given him. "I'm an Italian immigrant with a high school diploma," he admits. "[And] I am living the American dream."[2]

Many Contributions

Tommolillo is one of more than 46 million immigrants currently living in the United States. That translates to about 14 percent of the nation's population. The US-born children of these individuals constitute an additional 12 percent of the populace. According to the Migration Policy Institute, an organization that studies immigration, in total, the two groups account for about 80 million individuals.

The majority of Americans descend from immigrants. Since colonial times, people from all over the world have flocked to America in pursuit of freedom, opportunity, and equality. Many were met with hostility from individuals who claim that immigration hurts the nation. In fact, immigrants play a vital role in contributing to economic and social prosperity. They fill worker shortages, which increases productivity. And they start businesses that employ millions of workers. Indeed, nearly half of all *Fortune* 500 companies were started by immigrants or the children of immigrants. As a 2022 Massachusetts Institute of Technology (MIT) study asserts, "Immigrants act more as 'job creators' than 'job takers.'"[3]

Immigrants also support local communities and charitable organizations, enrich culture, and advance the arts, science, technology, and innovation. Immigrant inventors such as Alexander Graham Bell, who invented the telephone; Yvonne Brill, who invented a fuel-efficient jet propulsion system; Enrico Fermi, who invented the first nuclear reactor; Victor Ochoa, whose many inventions include an airplane with collapsible wings; and solar energy pioneer Maria Telkes can be found throughout US history. Immigrant innovators such as Elon Musk, who heads Tesla and founded Space X, and Sergey Brin, the cofounder of Google, continue to make a mark on the nation and the world. A 2022 National Bureau of Economic Research study found that inventors who are US immigrants produced nearly 25 percent of all new patents between 1990 and 2016 despite being only 16 percent of all US-based inventors.

Paying Their Way

Indeed, research and statistics suggest that immigrants contribute more to the economy than they receive in return. For example, undocumented immigrants (individuals who have entered the United States without proper authorization or have overstayed temporary visas) are not eligible to receive public benefits such as Medicaid, food stamps, or housing assistance. Yet they are required to pay taxes. According to New American Economy, an immigration research and advocacy organization, undocumented immigrants pay over $30 billion in federal, state, and local taxes annually. The National Immigration Law Center reports that "undocumented immigrants pay billions in taxes to fund programs they can't access."[4] About one-quarter of immigrants currently residing in the United States are undocumented.

Surrounded by family, an immigrant from Mexico (center) celebrates her naturalization as an American citizen. Research suggests that immigrants contribute far more to the economy than they receive in return.

In contrast, documented immigrants can access some, but not all, public benefit programs. Refugees, asylees (people who have been granted asylum), workers with extraordinary abilities, certain other skilled workers, and the immediate relatives of US citizens fall into this category. However, before any of these individuals can receive these benefits, they must maintain legal permanent resident status for at least five years. Moreover, according to the National Immigration Forum, even when documented immigrants meet these requirements, they use these programs at lower rates than their US-born peers.

Both documented and undocumented immigrants also contribute greatly to economic growth as consumers. Like almost all Americans, they rent and buy homes; shop for wants and needs; eat in restaurants; and go to movies, sporting events, and concerts. In fact, a 2019 American Community Survey found that immigrants exert $1.3 trillion in spending power per year.

Making the United States Great

Immigrants help make the United States great. As President Bill Clinton said in a 1998 commencement address at Portland State University,

More than any other nation on Earth, America has constantly drawn strength and spirit from wave after wave of immigrants. In each generation, they have proved to be the most restless, the most adventurous, the most innovative, the most industrious of people. Bearing different memories, honoring different heritages, they have strengthened our economy, enriched our culture, renewed our promise of freedom and opportunity for all.[5]

CHAPTER ONE

Hard Workers

In 2021, a group of elderly residents of a long-term care facility in Virginia helped ninety employees of the facility become naturalized US citizens. In gratitude for the attention and compassion shown to them by these immigrants, the residents raised enough money to pay each of their caregivers' citizenship application fees, which amounted to $725 per applicant. They also helped the workers study for their citizenship test and cheered them on at their swearing-in ceremony.

One-quarter of all long-term care facility workers in the United States are immigrants. They work long hours for low pay, at messy, physically demanding jobs. Many native-born Americans are reluctant to do these jobs. In fact, there is a national shortage of care workers. According to experts, without immigrants to fill these positions, it is likely that residents in nursing homes and other long-term care facilities would not receive proper care. As Robert Espinoza, vice president at PHI, an organization dedicated to improving long-term care, maintains, "Immigrants are critical to this workforce. . . . We think the industry would probably collapse without them."[6]

Filling Needs for Hundreds of Years

Since the nation's founding, immigrants have been instrumental in advancing the well-being of the United States and its people. Immigrants from all over the world have come to America in successive waves. In pursuit of a better life, they often take on jobs that native-born Americans are not eager to tackle but which are crucial to the nation's economic and social prosperity.

Even so, over the years, immigration has been a contentious political issue. And immigrants, especially those who are perceived as ethnically or culturally different from the general population, have faced prejudice and resentment. Nevertheless, each wave met these challenges head-on in pursuit of the American dream.

The first wave of immigrants arrived during the seventeenth and eighteenth centuries. It is not known how many people composed this wave. The vast majority were from the British Isles. Some came for adventure or the possibility of striking it rich. Many were fleeing religious persecution or poverty. Some of the poorest arrived as indentured servants contracting to work without compensation for a specified number of years in exchange for their sea passage. During the same period, an estimated 350,000 involuntary immigrants arrived from Africa. They were brought to America by force and sold as slaves. The United States would be a much different place without the contributions of all of these groups. They helped found the new nation, provide the labor that powered the economy of the South, and, in their quest for religious liberty, shape America's policy of religious freedom.

The next wave occurred between 1820 and 1870. More than 7 million people, mainly from northern Europe, were part of this wave. One-third were Irish people escaping famine in their homeland. Another 2 million came from Germany seeking a better life. Still others originated in Scandinavia. Sixty-three thousand Chinese immigrants, lured by tales of gold in California, were also part of this wave. The arrival of so many immigrants led to a big anti-immigration backlash. Irish and Chinese immigrants, in particular, encountered negative stereotypes, foul language, and overt discrimination.

A Positive Impact

Despite the backlash against such large numbers of people with unfamiliar cultures and customs, these nineteenth-century immigrants had a positive impact on the nation. They worked as manual laborers in fishing, logging, and mining as well as in factories and

on the railroads—all of which fueled the nation's transition to industrialization. Some even served in the military. Many German and Scandinavian immigrants settled rural areas in the Midwest, and some started businesses that contributed to the growth of cities such as Chicago and Milwaukee. German immigrants, for example, helped establish America's beer brewing industry, which is still thriving today.

Nonetheless, growing distrust toward ethnically different people led the government to create immigration quotas, which were designed to exclude people from Asia and Africa and radically decrease the arrival of people from southern and eastern Europe. Despite these limits, the late nineteenth and early twentieth centuries brought the largest wave of immigrants yet—approximately 30 million individuals. In contrast to the US Protestant majority, most were Catholics fleeing extreme poverty in Italy and Jews fleeing religious persecution in eastern Europe. Both groups were met with bigotry and abuse. Some Americans considered them dangerous. Many businesses refused to hire or serve them; they were banned from some educational institutions, and they were often denied housing.

Still, conditions in America were better than the conditions these individuals faced in Europe, and, like earlier immigrants, they helped advance American prosperity. They were essential in building the country's infrastructure, developing and advancing the garment industry, and starting businesses that still exist today. One such business, the Phillips-Van Heusen Shirt Company (now known as PVH), grew into one of the largest garment companies in the world. It was founded by a Jewish peddler named Moses Phillips, who made and sold flannel shirts to coal miners, many of whom were Irish immigrants.

Essential Workers Keep the Economy Moving

The fourth wave, which began after World War II, is ongoing. Political instability, crime, and lack of economic opportunity has brought 45 million immigrants—mainly from Latin America, the Caribbean, Asia, Africa, and the Middle East—to the United States. They, too, face open hostility from some Americans. Even so, like their predecessors, these immigrants provide the human resources for jobs that US citizens are unwilling or unqualified to do but which are essential to supporting society and keeping the economy moving. These positions are concentrated on either the high or low end of skill levels. Jobs in low-skill fields are often filled by undocumented immigrants who, lacking the proper documentation to be hired legally, take on almost any job they are offered. This often means working for unscrupulous employers under dangerous conditions for subsistence wages.

Low-end jobs are also filled by documented immigrants, no matter their skill level, due to discrimination, language and cultural barriers, or lack of US licenses and certificates. Sayed Ibrahim, a dentist and the founder of an oral care products company, recalls his experience: "I immigrated from the Sudan at the age of 28. I settled for minimum wage jobs even though I had a degree in chemistry and math. Those low-income jobs—like delivering pizza—put me in places where I got mugged, beaten up, and shot at multiple times."[7]

Jobs in the low-skill sector are generally low paying and involve hard physical labor. These positions tend to be in agriculture, fishing, forestry, construction, housekeeping, grounds maintenance, and caregiving—all occupational sectors in which there are, or would be, labor shortages without immigrants. In fact, the well-being of these sectors is linked to immigration. For instance, the American Farm Bureau Federation reports that over 2.4 million agricultural jobs must be filled each year. Farmers struggle to find workers to fill these positions. On average, wages are about 40 percent less than what other industries offer, and workers are expected to work long hours under poor conditions. They are exposed to pesticides linked to cancer as well as extreme weather conditions that can cause illness or death. Native-born Americans are not eager to take on these jobs. As Marty Yahner, who runs a beef farm in Pennsylvania, asserts, "Let's be brutally honest. Americans don't want to do manual labor. Not everybody can be a computer programmer. We still need the mechanics and the carpenters and the farmers and the truck drivers. Who the heck is going to run these farms and keep our world fed?"[8]

The answer is immigrants. Currently, over 73 percent of farmworkers are immigrants. About 3.8 million immigrants labor on farms and ranches as well as in slaughterhouses, food processing plants, grocery stores, and restaurants. The food production and distribution industries contribute more than $1.2 trillion per year to the gross domestic product, which is the total value of goods and services produced within a country in a specified period of time. Plus, the low wages that industry workers are paid keep domestic food prices down for American consumers. And during the COVID-19 pandemic, as essential workers, these immigrants helped keep the food supply chain open, even as parts of the food industry became hotbeds of contagion.

Highly Skilled Workers

Other immigrants fill high-skill jobs in fields that require specialized training, and they have done so for decades. Currently, immigrants are disproportionately represented in science, technology, engineering, and medicine. These are sectors in which the United States is not producing enough qualified people to fill the demand. For example, shortages of physicians, nurses, and pharmacists are widespread. And the lack of qualified medical professionals is projected to increase as the US population ages. According to the American Association of Medical Colleges, by 2033 the United States will face a shortage of up to 135,000 physicians. At the present time, one in five physicians is an immigrant. Many practice in underserved rural communities that would lack adequate health

The medical field has experienced shortages of physicians, nurses, and pharmacists. Immigrants are helping make up for this shortage. At present, one in five physicians in the United States is an immigrant.

care without their presence. Raghuveer Kura, an Indian-born kidney specialist who practices medicine in rural Missouri, explains: "I have 90 dialysis patients. I have to take care of the hospital all alone. . . . [Without me] people will die because there's nobody to do their dialysis."[9]

Like Kura, most high-skilled immigrants also have strong education credentials. Approximately 47 percent of recent immigrants earned a bachelor's degree or higher before arriving in the United States, and more than half of all doctoral degree holders are immigrants. Some are recruited in their home countries by US universities and private companies. Others come to the United States for higher education and are hired by US employers upon their graduation. Charles Elachi, an immigrant from Lebanon, followed the latter path. The former director of the Jet Propulsion Lab (JPL) at the National Aeronautics and Space Administration supervised the launch of twenty-four missions, including the first successful Mars landing. Before being hired by the JPL, he attended graduate school in California, where he earned three master's degrees and a doctorate. "My studies and degrees landed me a job at JPL in 1970," he explains. "In science and engineering, where people try new things and solve problems, they don't ask where you're from. . . . Your mind and your ideas—those are the things that matter."[10] Nevertheless, under US law, employers must try to fill vacant positions with US citizens before they can recruit and hire foreign-born workers.

Once hired, highly skilled immigrants bring valuable abilities to the labor force that advance society, spur innovation, and enhance the nation's global reputation. The National Academy of Sciences reports that approximately one-third of US Nobel Prize winners in chemistry, medicine, and physics are scientists who immigrated to the United States. These talented individuals are

Coming to the United States

Throughout history, immigrants have faced many challenges while coming to the United States. America's earliest immigrants spent months crossing the Atlantic Ocean on barely seaworthy sailing ships, where disease spread rapidly. Many died before reaching land.

The shift to steam-powered vessels made the transatlantic voyage faster but not necessarily more pleasant. Many nineteenth- and early twentieth-century immigrants shared shipboard living and sleeping accommodations with as many as one thousand other individuals, and sickness was common. Upon their arrival, the newcomers were inspected by immigration officials. If they were ill or deemed unable to earn a living, they were shipped back to their native country.

The passage of restrictive immigration laws presents even more challenges for modern immigrants. Obtaining a visa to legally enter the United States is difficult. Lacking proper documentation, many immigrants hike through miles of desert without adequate food or water, hoping to slip unnoticed across the southern border. Some die en route. Others are taken into custody by the border patrol and are deported.

responsible for many of the cutting edge ideas and technologies that have improved the lives of people throughout the world. Moreover, immigrants are more likely than their American peers to obtain a patent that is used commercially. For instance, James Hillier, a Canadian immigrant who developed the first commercially successful electron microscope, was granted forty-one US patents during his career. His inventions helped his employer, RCA, grow and flourish.

The work of inventive immigrants like Hillier drives long-term economic growth. Their inventions raise their employers' revenues, which helps increase dividend payments to stockholders, augments funding for new research and development, and boosts the hiring of more workers. As Harvard Business School professor William Kerr notes, "Immigration has been a tremendous boost to science and engineering. . . . High-skilled immigration is fundamentally an investment."[11]

Entrepreneurs

In addition to filling existing jobs, immigrants create new businesses and, in the process, jobs for others. Immigrants are risk-takers.

Immigration and Population Growth

The US population is aging, and the birth rate is decreasing. When combined, these factors can lead to a decrease in the population, which can negatively impact economic growth. Without an adequate supply of working-age individuals to fill jobs vacated by older workers, the workforce shrinks and productivity and revenues decline. According to the US Census Bureau, keeping the immigration level high can counteract these factors because immigrants and their children are typically younger than the rest of the population. Nonetheless, many Americans want to curtail immigration.

Future national population projections, however, suggest this policy is a mistake. Even a small decrease in immigration levels can hurt the economy. As William H. Frey of the Brookings Institution writes,

> Although the U.S. faces population growth and aging challenges in the decades ahead, we are still in a better position than many other developed countries . . . due in large part to the healthy immigration levels we experienced over the past 30 to 40 years. . . . In a future of decreasing births and increasing deaths across an already aging population, immigration levels are crucial in leading to national growth as opposed to decline.

William H. Frey, "New Census Projections Show Immigration Is Essential to the Growth and Vitality of a More Diverse US Population," Brookings Institution, November 29, 2023. www.brookings.edu.

On the chance that they will gain a better life, they often leave their loved ones and possessions behind. They travel long distances, often under dangerous circumstances, to come to a country where they might be unfamiliar with the language and culture—and where they are not always welcomed. There are no guarantees that their efforts will pay off, yet they are willing to run the risk. Similarly, starting a new business requires a high tolerance for risk, especially since half of all new businesses fail within five years, according to the Bureau of Labor Statistics.

Therefore, it is not surprising that as risk-takers, immigrants are willing to take a chance and start a business in pursuit of the American dream. Take Barry Zhang as an example. He emigrated from China in 1987 to study at Princeton University, where he earned doctorates in two engineering fields. Shortly after graduating, he started a fiber optics manufacturing firm, which has grown to employ more than eighty workers and produce $10 million in revenue. He explains, "It's in my blood. I never thought about finding a job—I just wanted to do something on my own. . . . By definition [immigrants are] more risk taking. It's always been true—all these generations of immigrants, from the very beginning, they've always been harder working and more willing to take risks than people who've been here a generation or two or longer."[12]

Racism and discrimination also play a role in why immigrants, especially immigrants of color, start businesses. Throughout US history, immigrants have often faced discrimination in the workforce. They are frequently forced to toil at jobs for which they are vastly overqualified or for employers who take advantage of their immigrant status. Rather than labor in these positions long term, some start their own businesses.

Although immigrants compose only 14 percent of the population, they make up 21 percent of all business owners in the United States. According to a 2022 MIT study, per capita, immigrants are about 80 percent more likely than native-born Americans to start a new business. On average, these businesses employ 1 percent more workers than those founded by US natives.

Small and Large Businesses

Many of these businesses are small retail shops, restaurants, and personal service firms offering goods and services that meet the needs of local communities. During the nineteenth century, for instance, many Chinese immigrants opened laundries and restaurants that filled the needs of California miners. Likewise, since the late twentieth century, Vietnamese American entrepreneurs have dominated the nail salon industry, and many Indian immigrants have opened truck stop and gas station restaurants.

Some of these small businesses have grown into *Fortune* 500 companies. Capital One, DoorDash, DuPont, Levi Strauss, Oscar Mayer, Pfizer, and US Steel are just a few *Fortune* 500 giants started by immigrants. Indeed, the American Immigration Council reports that 44.8 percent of all *Fortune* 500 companies were founded by immigrants or their children. These companies have contributed much to the economy at the local, state, and national levels, as well as to America's global standing. As a group, *Fortune* 500 companies started by immigrants or their children employ more than 14.8 million people worldwide and earn $8.1 trillion in revenue annually.

Immigrants are also responsible for creating high-tech start-up firms that are currently worth billions—and, in some cases, trillions—of dollars. A 2022 analysis by the National Foundation for American Policy found that more than half of US start-up companies valued at $1 billion or more were started by immigrants. For instance, Oxford Economics reports that in 2022 YouTube, whose founders include Taiwanese immigrant Steve Chen and German immigrant Jawed Karim, contributed $35 billion to the

High-tech companies such as YouTube have contributed greatly to the US economy. Its founders are Taiwanese immigrant Steve Chen (left), German immigrant Jawed Karim (right), and American-born Chad Hurley (center).

US gross national product. The report goes on to say that the company supported jobs for more than 390,000 people. Google, which was cofounded by Russian Jewish immigrant Sergey Brin, employs more than ten thousand people in North America. In addition, Google has stated that the company's advertising tools produced approximately $400 billion of economic activity for more than 2 million American businesses in 2020.

Indeed, from the early immigrants who helped settle America to today's greatest innovators, immigrants have proved themselves to be essential to America's prosperity. For hundreds of years, they have taken on tough jobs, enhanced productivity, and helped the nation grow. While president, John F. Kennedy wrote, "Every aspect of the American economy has profited from the contributions of immigrants."[13]

CHAPTER TWO

Building and Connecting Communities

During the 1990s, a civil war in Somalia brought thousands of Somali refugees to the United States. Large numbers settled in Minnesota. They were drawn to the region by employment opportunities in the meat processing industry, affordable housing, and the presence of other Somali immigrants in the area. As If-rah Jimale, one of these Somali immigrants, explains, "Some of the things I was told about Minnesota and why I should move here were that jobs were plentiful, that I could go to school if I wanted, and that I would always find cheap housing. And there were many nonprofit organizations and other Somalis who would help me with any other issues."[14]

According to Minnesota Compass, an organization that tracks data about Minnesota communities, more than eighty-six thousand Somali Americans currently live in Minnesota, composing the largest Somali community outside of Somalia. These individuals have played an important role in both Minne-sota's and Minneapolis's growth and prosperity. Somali-owned businesses have revitalized neglected sections of that city. And Somali immigrants have boosted the state's otherwise declining population, grown the economy, and shaped area politics. In a 2023 speech, Minnesota governor Tim Walz acknowledged these contributions, declaring, "Minnesota thrives because of the Somali community."[15]

Establishing Thriving Communities

Indeed, immigrants, like those in Minnesota, have always played a major role in building American communities, both literally and figuratively. They have helped develop, enrich, revitalize, and lead large and small communities all across the nation. Immigrants tend to settle and cluster in urban areas where there are employment and educational opportunities and where housing is cheap and plentiful. They also tend to settle in neighborhoods where other individuals who share their language and culture reside. Living near others who share a common culture, language, and challenges provides new arrivals with a support network, no matter how much hostility they may face from some Americans or how different the local culture might be. In fact, the presence of immigrants in a region acts like a magnet that attracts others with a similar background.

As more immigrants move into an area, cultural and ethnic enclaves develop. These usually form in undeveloped or declining sections of host cities and towns. To serve the new residents, businesses; restaurants; and social, religious, and civic organizations open. Vacant homes gain occupants, and new construction arises. Consequently, new employment opportunities are created. As a result, even more newcomers flock to the area, and these enclaves grow into thriving communities whose existence boosts and enriches the local economy and culture. This is what happened in Orlando, Florida, and Las Vegas, Nevada. Large numbers of immigrants helped transform these and other once-small cities into prosperous metropolitan areas, says Nancy Foner, professor of sociology at City University of New York's Hunter College.

Flushing, Queens, is another example of a flourishing community that followed this growth pattern. Naresh, an Indian immigrant who arrived in New York City during the 1960s, has been a longtime resident of Flushing. Upon arriving in New York, he settled in an established Indian American enclave in the borough of Manhattan.

"Minnesota thrives because of the Somali community."[15]

—Tim Walz, governor of Minnesota

Somali refugees who settled in Minnesota have contributed to state and local growth and prosperity. A Somali immigrant shop owner (far right) is among those who have helped revitalize neighborhoods.

However, the neighborhood was overcrowded, and the rents were high. So, once Naresh adjusted to his new life, he looked for a more desirable area to live. He found it in Flushing. The area was sparsely populated at the time, making housing cheap. And it was only a few subways stops from his workplace and former neighborhood. He recalls, "I was satisfied with Flushing because . . . the apartment rents were quite cheap. At the time, every third plot in Flushing was vacant."[16]

Although there were only a few other Indian Americans living in Flushing when Naresh settled there, it did not take long for some of Naresh's friends and family, as well as other Indian immigrants, to join him. By the 1980s, the neighborhood had grown into a prosperous ethnic community. Several Indian houses of worship were constructed, including the second-oldest Hindu temple in the United States, and Indian-owned stores, restaurants, and businesses filled almost every block.

Asian immigrants have played a key role in the growth and prosperity of the borough of Queens as a whole. Since the 1980s, the borough's population has increased by 25 percent, largely due to the influx of Indian, Chinese, and Korean immigrants. As of 2023, immigrants make up approximately half of the borough's labor force, according to the Office of the New York State Comptroller.

Immigrant communities, like that in Flushing, exist throughout the United States. The largest and oldest are in, or close to, large metropolitan areas. San Francisco's and New York City's Chinatowns are among the most famous of these communities. Both were established during the nineteenth century, and both still serve as home to thousands of Chinese Americans. Little Havana, a neighborhood in downtown Miami, is another flourishing ethnic community established by immigrants. It developed during the 1960s as a refuge for Cuban exiles and has grown to be home to about fifty thousand people, most of whom are Cuban and other Hispanic immigrants.

Immigrants also established and expanded communities in rural areas and in small cities and towns. They played a big role in America's westward expansion. During the nineteenth century, the federal government offered cheap land to families willing to farm undeveloped western lands that the government wanted settled. Thousands of Norwegian immigrants took advantage of this offer. They were instrumental in cultivating large sections of the Great Plains and upper Midwest, an area known as America's breadbasket. In doing so, they helped feed the growing nation. Similarly, eighteenth-century Spanish settlers established small communities across the Southwest. Over the centuries, Mexican immigrants turned these enclaves into thriving cities such as El Paso, Los Angeles, and Santa Fe, among others.

Connecting Communities

In addition to establishing and expanding communities, immigrants play a vital role in physically building and connecting communities. Immigrant architects, engineers, and laborers have designed and built residential and commercial buildings, roads, rail systems, canals, bridges, and tunnels throughout the nation. Their efforts made it faster, easier, and cheaper to move people, goods, and services around the continent, thereby spurring economic growth and enhancing quality of life.

Irish immigrants, for example, played an oversized role in constructing the many canals that connect America's inland and port cities. Using shovels and pickaxes, more than three thousand Irish laborers were largely responsible for digging the 363-mile-long (584 km) trench that formed the Erie Canal. Completed in 1825, it was the first navigable waterway to connect the Great Lakes to the Atlantic Ocean. Its opening accelerated the arrival of settlers to the upper Midwest, which sped up the region's growth and the westward expansion of the United States. In 1820, the combined population of Illinois, Indiana, Michigan, and Ohio was about 800,000. By 1850, that number had grown to more than 4 million. Historians attribute this growth primarily to the opening of the canal.

The success of the Erie Canal led to the construction of other canals. By 1860, more than 4,000 miles (6,437 km) of canals spread across the United States. Most were dug by Irish immigrants, many of whom sacrificed their lives in the process, dying in accidents or from infectious diseases that spread like wildfire through worker encampments. Describing the dangerous conditions, this is what one nineteenth-century Irish canal laborer wrote to his sister: "I don't know, dear Sister, if any of us will survive. . . . Six of me tentmates died this very day and were stacked like cordwood until they could be taken away."[17]

Irish immigrants were also instrumental in the construction of the transcontinental railroad during the 1860s, which linked the United States from east to west. Likewise, an estimated fifteen to twenty thousand Chinese laborers toiled long hours doing dangerous and backbreaking work. Through the efforts of these immigrants, travel time across the United States went from months to under a week. Consequently, vast regions of the country were open to more rapid development—leading to a growth in trade.

Creating National Parks

John Muir was a boy when his family came to the United States from Scotland in 1849. The family settled on a farm in Wisconsin, where Muir developed a great interest in nature. To learn about America's wildlands, in 1867 he undertook a 1,000-mile (1,609 km) trek from Indiana to Florida's Gulf Coast, documenting the plants and animals he saw. A year later, he headed west to explore California's Yosemite Valley and Sierra Nevada range. During his exploration, he climbed mountains, scaled cliffs, and kept a record of the area's plants, animals, and geology. Next, he headed north to Alaska, where he measured the movement of glaciers.

Muir was passionate about preserving America's forests. He founded the Sierra Club to help protect the environment, and he urged the government to ban commercial exploitation of designated wildlands. He wrote many books and articles detailing his explorations and promoting his conservationist views, which influenced many powerful people in government. Indeed, by 1916, eight new national parks were established, mainly due to his influence. Muir's contributions made it possible for millions of Americans to enjoy and take pride in the country's natural wonders.

Irish immigrants, along with Italian immigrants, can also take credit for building important infrastructure—including subway networks and vehicular tunnels and bridges—that connected American cities and states. But it was a German immigrant, John Roebling, who invented a way to make wire rope, which made the construction of some of America's iconic suspension bridges possible. Roebling was a German engineer who settled in a German American enclave in Pennsylvania in 1831. After a failed attempt at farming, he turned his attention to fabricating rope from wire, which he believed could be used in the construction of suspension bridges. Roebling patented his design, and in 1848 he opened a factory in Trenton, New Jersey, that manufactured wire rope. His invention made him very wealthy, and the business he founded, John A. Roebling's Sons Company, was the largest employer in Trenton for many decades.

Roebling designed several bridges in Pennsylvania and New York, including the Brooklyn Bridge, which may be the most famous suspension bridge in the world. When he died in 1869, before construction of the Brooklyn Bridge began, his son, Washington

John Roebling, a German immigrant and civil engineer, designed New York City's Brooklyn Bridge (pictured). His Trenton, New Jersey, factory manufactured the wire rope used in suspension bridges like this one and provided jobs to many people for decades.

Roebling, directed the project. Immigrants from all over the world performed the actual manual labor. Scores were killed in accidents during the bridge's construction.

The bridge opened in 1883. By connecting the boroughs of Brooklyn and Manhattan, it improved the quality of life for many New Yorkers. Before the bridge was built, the only way to commute between the two boroughs was by boat. The opening of the bridge made it easy for people to commute to jobs in Manhattan from Brooklyn, which spurred the growth of Brooklyn. Even today, more than a century since its opening, the bridge remains an important part of American life. According to the New York City Department of Transportation, an estimated 117,000 vehicles and 30,000 pedestrians cross it every day.

Revitalizing Communities

Immigrants have also helped revitalize communities with shrinking populations and economies. New American Economy reports that from 2014 to 2017, immigrants contributed about 33 percent of the total population growth in the nation's one hundred top metropolitan areas. This is important because population growth fuels economic growth, whereas population loss leads to economic decay. Without the influx of immigrants, the populations of major cities such as Detroit, Philadelphia, and St. Louis would have decreased considerably, and some small towns might have disappeared. In Philadelphia, for example, it is estimated that by 2017 the city's population would have declined by more than thirteen thousand people without an influx of immigrants. Instead, due to the city's welcoming practices toward newcomers and the relatively low cost of housing compared to other large cities, the population grew by about forty-seven thousand people.

Generally, communities decline when a major industry shuts down, causing many unemployed residents to move to areas where jobs are more plentiful. With fewer customers, local businesses lose income and are forced to close. As a result, the local tax base plummets. Lack of adequate tax revenue hampers the community's ability to fund basic services, which, in turn, causes more people to leave. Therefore, apartments and houses become vacant, and home sales fall.

When immigrants move into these depressed areas, they help revitalize them. They buy and rent houses and apartments, which raises property values. They support existing businesses and open new ones, creating jobs and spurring investment in the community. And they pay taxes and enrich the local culture. Immigrants, says Jennifer Van Hook, professor of sociology and demography at Pennsylvania State University, "are consumers. They come in, end up buying groceries, buying houses, and manage to keep the market going in these places where otherwise there wouldn't be much demand."[18]

Turning Detroit Around

One city that was revitalized by immigrants is Detroit. A downturn in the city's manufacturing and auto industries during the late twentieth and early twenty-first centuries prompted many residents to leave the area, which devastated the city and its tax base. Homes and businesses were boarded up, essential services were cut, and crime increased. Some neighborhoods were like ghost towns. Detroit's economy declined so drastically that the city filed for bankruptcy in 2013. When large numbers of Middle Eastern, Hispanic, Asian, and African immigrants started moving to the

Immigrants such as this café owner from Yemen have helped transform the Detroit area in the last decade. Once-dilapidated neighborhoods and abandoned businesses are rebounding and flourishing.

area around 2014, the city started to rebound. These newcomers transformed dilapidated neighborhoods, reopened abandoned shopping malls, started more than one thousand new business-es, created hundreds of jobs, stimulated the housing market, and paid millions of dollars in taxes.

Tracey Garley, a Liberian refugee, is one of these individuals who helped turn Detroit around. She opened a boutique clothing store in downtown Detroit in 2014. It was the first new clothing store to open in Detroit since the city filed for bankruptcy. Deter-mined to make the business a success and, at the same time, reenergize the downtown area, she posted positive things about Detroit on Instagram. And, with other immigrant entrepreneurs, she hosted pop-up events that drew people downtown and en-couraged other new businesses to open nearby. Garley has since started other businesses; she also founded and serves as the chief executive officer (CEO) of a nonprofit organization that offers internships for prospective entrepreneurs so that they, too, can help grow Detroit and other US cities.

Leading and Serving Communities

Immigrants not only build and revitalize communities but also help cities, states, and the nation prosper by serving as com-munity leaders and public servants, and they have done so since the nation's founding. Eight of the original fifty-six signers of the Declaration of Independence were foreign born, as were four of the nation's first six secretaries of the treasury. In all, twenty-three immigrants have held US cabinet positions. Among them were Irish-born James McHenry, who was appointed secretary of war in 1796 by George Washington, and Cuban-born Alejandro May-orkas, who was appointed to the post of secretary of homeland security by Joe Biden in 2021. Two immigrants, Henry Kissinger, who emigrated from Germany, and Madeleine Albright, who emi-grated from Czechoslovakia (now the Czech Republic), served as secretary of state. This is one of the highest-ranking cabinet posts in the government. Albright was a child when her family came to the United States in 1948. She was the first woman ever to hold the office. Albright also served as the US ambassador to the United Nations.

Many other immigrants and their children have also held elected office. According to federal law, US presidents and vice presidents must be native-born citizens. But naturalized citizens who have lived in the country for a set number of years are eligible to serve in the US Senate and House of Representatives. According to the Pew Research Center, 14 percent of the 117th US Congress are immigrants or the children of immigrants.

Naturalized citizens can also hold state and municipal offices. Since the eighteenth century, seventy-two foreign-born individuals have served as governors. Actor, businessman, and former professional bodybuilder Arnold Schwarzenegger is one of the most well-known. He served as the governor of California from 2003 to 2011. Schwarzenegger grew up in a Soviet-occupied region of Austria. His family was very poor—so poor, in fact, that his mother often went door-to-door begging for food. He started weight training when he was fifteen years old in hopes of escaping poverty

Military Service

Since the United States' founding, immigrants have served in the US military, risking their lives in service to their adopted homeland. Immigrants fought in the Civil War and World War I and II, as well as in Korea, Vietnam, Afghanistan, and Iraq. They have fought honorably, with many being awarded the military's highest honor, the Medal of Honor. Immigrants have served in wartime and peacetime. An estimated forty-five thousand immigrants are actively serving in the US military today, according to FWD, a bipartisan organization that advocates for immigration reform. Moreover, the government estimates that five thousand immigrants enlist every year.

Some immigrants have even fought for the United States before being granted citizenship. In reward for their service, noncitizens who have completed at least one year of honorable service are eligible to become naturalized citizens. Many have obtained citizenship this way. US Marine lance corporal Jose Gutierrez, an immigrant from Guatemala, was one of the first American troops to lose his life in Iraq. He was killed in a 2003 tank battle. Gutierrez was not a US citizen when he died. He was awarded citizenship shortly after his death.

by becoming a professional bodybuilder. Five years later, in 1967, he became the youngest person in history to win the title of Mr. Universe. Shortly thereafter, he was given the opportunity to train in California, and he took it. Although he had no money and did not speak English, he was determined to succeed, and by working hard, he did. In the process, like millions of other immigrants, he helped build the nation. As he explained in a 2004 speech, "I arrived here with empty pockets but full of dreams, full of determination, full of desire. . . . Everything I have, my career, my success, my family, I owe to America. . . . No matter the nationality, no matter the religion, no matter the ethnic background, America brings out the best in people."[19] Indeed, communities across the nation owe a lot to the millions of immigrants who have given their best to build and strengthen their new homeland.

—Arnold Schwarzenegger, immigrant and former governor of California

CHAPTER THREE

Enriching American Culture

St. Patrick's Day is one of the most widely celebrated holidays in the United States. The holiday was originally observed as a solemn holy day in Ireland. But it evolved into a spirited secular celebration in the United States thanks to Irish American immigrants. During the eighteenth and nineteenth centuries, Irish immigrants faced negative stereotypes and mistreatment from many Americans. To display their strength, exhibit pride in their heritage, and highlight their contributions to their new homeland, Irish Americans threw parties and held parades on St. Patrick's Day. Doing so also served as a way for them to gain acceptance and lessen the bias against them. According to Elizabeth Stack, the executive director of the Irish American Heritage Museum in Albany, New York, "You had parades of men who were policemen and in the Army and the Navy and sanitation marching up Fifth Avenue. It was a demonstration of their voting power as an immigrant group, but also it showed their willingness to serve and to be part of the fabric of American political and city life."[20]

Over the years, the parties, celebrations, and parades have grown bigger and bigger as Americans of every background adopted the holiday as a mainstream celebration. About sixty US cities hold St. Patrick's Day parades. New York City's parade is the largest in the world, attracting an estimated 2 million spectators each year. Celebrants all over the United States dress in green, drink green beer, eat festive meals, and pin shamrocks to their lapels. The city of Chicago dyes the Chicago River green to mark the occasion.

Not only do these festivities enrich American culture, they also stimulate the economy. The National Retail Federation reports that Americans spend more than $5 billion a year on the holiday. They host parties; flock to restaurants and bars; and buy special foods, beverages, clothes, decorations, and souvenirs. Revelers use taxis and rideshares, and tourists fill hotels in parade cities.

Sharing Celebrations

St. Patrick's Day is just one of several cultural celebrations that immigrant groups brought to the United States. They blended their traditions and customs with American culture to form new hybrid celebrations. These celebrations help Americans of different cultural and ethnic backgrounds connect with one another, which contributes to social and economic prosperity. As President

St. Patrick's Day parades, like this one in New York City, are an example of immigrants (in this case, from Ireland) blending their traditions with American culture to create something new that anyone can enjoy.

Lyndon B. Johnson said, upon signing the 1965 Immigration and Nationality Act, "The land flourished because it was fed from so many sources—because it was nourished by so many cultures and traditions and peoples."[21]

Like St. Patrick's Day, Lunar New Year (also known as Chinese New Year) festivities have long been a part of American life. The holiday has been celebrated in communities with large Asian populations since the 1860s. In fact, the celebration in San Francisco is the largest in the world outside of Asia. It includes a huge parade with floats and costumed revelers performing lion and dragon dances, a beauty pageant, a fireworks display, and a huge flower market. About one hundred thousand vendors line the parade route, and celebrants buy new clothes for the occasion, exchange symbolic gifts, travel to family gatherings, and host banquets. The festivities attract hundreds of thousands of tourists and generate millions of dollars in revenue for local businesses.

Moreover, sharing the holiday with friends and acquaintances of diverse backgrounds helps individuals better understand each other. Thomas, a Vietnamese American, for example, makes a point of inviting people of different cultures to his family's Lunar New Year banquet. "We all look for times of the year that we can have a reason to come together and be thankful and remember things and commune with our friends and eat good food," he says. "Luckily, my culture brings another day into the mix."[22] In this small way, Thomas is helping combat the negative stereotypes and prejudice that, throughout US history, was often directed toward Asian Americans.

Quinceañeras and b'nai mitzvahs, rites of passage that were brought to the United States by Hispanic and Jewish immigrants, respectively, also enrich American culture while contributing to economic prosperity. Quinceañeras, which are associated with Catholicism and Hispanic culture, celebrate a fifteen-year-old girl's transition from girlhood to womanhood. Similarly, b'nai mitzvahs celebrate a thirteen-year-old child's transition to adulthood. Both events begin with religious ceremonies followed by a celebratory reception. Many of these receptions have evolved from small family parties to elaborate revelries in which the food, music, rituals, and decor reflect and honor the celebrant's foreign and American heritage.

Approximately 525,000 quinceañeras and 73,000 b'nai mitzvahs are held in the United States annually. Hosts spend an average of $10,000 to $20,000 on these coming-of-age parties. Their popularity has created whole industries that produce huge revenues and employ millions of people. Juan Briones,

Quinceañeras, a tradition brought to the United States by Hispanic immigrants, enrich American culture and contribute to the prosperity of the many businesses that provide services to make the event special.

the Mexican American owner of a choreography business, is one of these people. His business provides dance instructions for quinceañera celebrants. "So many people live off of this industry: DJs, the cake maker, decorations, the people who sell dresses, rent the tuxedos, the ones who do photography and video, those of us who do the choreography, people who make invitations, musicians, bands," he explains. "All of these services profit from the fiestas. Quinceañeras move the money around our community."[23] Moreover, participating in or learning about these and other special ethnic events helps Americans better understand people of different backgrounds.

Ethnic Foods Are American Foods

Every celebration is accompanied by food and drinks. Food links people with their cultural roots and exposes individuals of diverse backgrounds to other cultures. One of the best ways for people to learn about different cultures is through food. Immigrants introduced foods from their homelands to the United States, and they created new recipes by adapting their native dishes to accommodate local ingredients and American tastes. *Forbes* reports

Cinco de Mayo

Cinco de Mayo is a Mexican holiday that commemorates Mexico's victory over French rule in 1862. The holiday was brought to the United States by Mexican immigrants to celebrate their heritage, highlight their contributions to US culture and history, and connect with other Americans. Currently, the holiday is more widely celebrated in the United States than it is in Mexico.

On May 5 (Cinco de Mayo) each year, communities with a large Mexican American presence hold parades, street fairs, and public festivals featuring food trucks, entertainment, handicrafts, lowrider car shows, and Mexican-style wrestling matches. Large cities such as Chicago, Los Angeles, and San Antonio, to name a few, host huge celebrations. Los Angeles's celebration is the largest in the world, and San Antonio's lasts an entire week.

Cinco de Mayo celebrations enrich American culture. They also add to economic growth. According to the US Distilled Spirits Council, sales of tequila and Mexican beer rise significantly in the days leading up to the holiday. So do the sales of avocados used to make guacamole, a Mexican dip. In addition, restaurants and bars spend millions of dollars on promoting holiday specials.

that American cuisine is the most diverse in the world. Eateries serving Chinese, Italian, Mexican, and Thai foods, to name just a few cuisines, can be found all over the United States. According to author and social historian Paul Freedman, there are more Chinese restaurants in the United States than there are McDonald's, Burger King, and KFC restaurants combined. Many ethnic food eateries are owned and operated by immigrants, as are thousands of ethnic grocery stores.

David Leong is an immigrant and restaurant owner. He came to the United States from China in 1940. After serving in the US military during World War II, he opened a Chinese restaurant in Springfield, Missouri. The traditional Chinese dishes he served did not appeal to local tastes. In contrast, a local eatery that featured fried chicken with gravy was always busy. So, to attract customers, he put an original spin on a traditional Chinese chicken dish by breading and deep frying the chicken, adding "gravy" made with Chinese condiments, and topping the dish with cashew nuts. He named his creation Springfield Cashew Chicken after his adopted hometown. The dish became a staple in the area.

Leong is not alone. Every immigrant group has introduced Americans to new foods and new ways to cook food. Hot dogs, pizza, potato salad, nachos, lasagna, and pretzels are just a few of the hundreds of foods that immigrants introduced to the American table. Ethnic foods are so much a part of mainstream American culture that supermarkets across the nation reserve large sections for ethnic food products. And major corporations such as General Mills and Conagra manufacture ready-to-eat ethnic food products that reach a global market. Indeed, the ethnic food industry has contributed greatly to the national economy. According to market research, the US ethnic food industry earned $42.9 billion in 2022 and is expected to grow to $106.5 billion by 2032. Moreover, it has enriched American culture, reflecting the nation's multicultural roots and making life in the United States more flavorful.

Creators and Consumers of Popular Culture

Immigrants also impact American social and economic prosperity as both consumers and producers of pop culture. Immigrants and their children have created many new forms of entertainment. As with so many other industries, much of the success of America's entertainment industry can be credited to immigrants. During the early twentieth century, immigrant entrepreneurs such as Carl Laemmle, Louis B. Mayer, and Harry Warner played a huge role in building the Hollywood film industry. They founded Hollywood film studios that grew into thriving megastudios. Moreover, immigrants and the children of immigrants played a huge role in writing, producing, directing, and acting in some of the most successful films ever made. By making movies that portray American values and the United States as a land of opportunity, these films touched the hearts and minds of viewers—no matter their place of birth. Moreover, the popularity of classic and new films contributes greatly to the nation's economic growth. According to the career website Zippia, the movie industry adds more than $500 billion per year to America's gross domestic product. It employs more than 2 million people and produces one of the country's most profitable and sought-after exports.

The contribution of immigrants to the music industry has had a similar impact on American social and economic success. A 2021 report by Economists Incorporated states that the industry contributes $170 billion to the US gross domestic product annually and supports 2.5 million jobs. Many songs that became American classics were written during the early twentieth century by immigrants and the children of immigrants. Irving Berlin is one of the most well-known. He was a Jewish immigrant who arrived in the United States from Russia in 1893 at the age of five. Growing up in poverty, he became a busker, singing on street corners to earn money. Although he never learned to read music, with the help of music transcribers he composed the scores and lyrics for an estimated fifteen hundred songs. Several of his songs, such as

"God Bless America" and "White Christmas," are timeless symbols of American culture. In fact, "God Bless America" has been called the nation's second national anthem. It was sung on the steps of the US Capitol by members of Congress after the 2001 terrorist attacks on New York City and Washington, DC. Berlin would have approved of its use. He often said that he wrote the song to express his love of and gratitude to his new homeland.

More recently, by fusing American pop music with music from their native lands, immigrants from the Caribbean and Latin America have taken American music in new directions. Caribbean immigrant superstars such as Rihanna and Nicki Minaj, for instance, have fused reggae and other island sounds with American hip hop and rap. The resulting music stretches musical boundaries, forming fresh and catchy tunes that have gained popularity with

Rihanna performs during the Super Bowl halftime show in 2023. An immigrant from Barbados, her music blends Caribbean rhythms, hip hop, rhythm and blues, electronic beats, and rock.

people of diverse cultures and backgrounds. These artists' influence also extends to the world of fashion. Both women are icons and role models for young American women who admire and imitate their sense of style.

Hispanic immigrants, such as Carlos Santana, have also enriched American culture. Santana, who was born and raised in Mexico, is considered by many to be one of the most innovative guitarists in the world. His music, an Afro-Latin-blues-rock blend, resulted in a new sound whose music and lyrics celebrate and emphasize the importance of unity between diverse cultures. Indeed, without these artists and others like them, American music would not be the same. According to music critic Howard Reich, "The template for American music, a cacophonous merger of a thousand cultures thrown together like nowhere on earth, is built on the shoulders of immigrants."[24]

Foreign-Language Skills and Cultural Diversity

As creators of pop culture, immigrants frequently use more than one language in their work. In fact, being bilingual and bicultural are other ways immigrants contribute to national prosperity. Immigrants bring their native languages and culture with them. Some are fluent in English when they arrive; others become bilingual over time. The Pew Research Center reports that 47 percent of all immigrants speak English well within five years of immigrating, and most second-generation immigrants are bilingual. In contrast, a survey conducted by Preply, an online language-tutoring site, found that most US students study a foreign language briefly in high school but forget what they learned within a year. As a result, monolingual Americans miss out on many opportunities.

Bilingual, culturally diverse workers are in high demand throughout the workforce, and the demand keeps growing. For example, according to New American Economy, there were approximately 240,000 job postings aimed at bilingual workers in 2010. That number increased to 630,000 by 2015—and that number continues to grow. Moreover, the US Department of La-

Kosher and Halal Foods

Observant Jewish and Muslim people follow strict religious dietary laws. These laws forbid the mixing of meat and dairy products as well as the consumption of certain foods, such as pork and pork products, carnivorous animals, and animals that are killed in an unethical manner. Foods that are permitted in Jewish dietary laws are said to be kosher, and those permitted in Muslim dietary laws are said to be halal.

Kosher and halal foods are sold throughout the United States. According to the Orthodox Union, an organization that certifies kosher foods, more than 12 million Americans purchase kosher foods annually. These sales generate about $12 billion. Similarly, Islamic Services of America, an organization that certifies halal foods, reports that Americans spend about $20 billion annually on halal foods. And the demand is projected to increase as America's Muslim community grows. Moreover, many Americans prefer these products for health and safety reasons, as do people concerned with the ethical treatment of animals.

bor reports that the demand for interpreters and translators is expected to increase by 24 percent through 2030, which is much faster than the average job growth for other occupations. And the demand cuts across a variety of industries. Market research company Gitnux found that in 2023, 60 percent of job listings on LinkedIn required bilingual candidates. Without immigrants and their offspring, many of these positions would go unfilled.

Such positions can be found throughout the United States. Businesses and public agencies located in communities with a large immigrant presence need bilingual workers. Being bilingual allows teachers, social workers, police officers, and health care workers, among others, to communicate and build trust with community members who are not proficient in English. It also boosts sales at local businesses. As Laura Fuentes, of internet service provider Infinity Dish, notes, "Relying solely on English-only employees means missing out on a lucrative portion of the market and denying accessible customer support to a large number of your clients. Point blank, we couldn't conduct business at the level we want without our multilingual employees."[25]

US-based multinational companies also benefit from these workers. With the growth of globalization, big businesses are seeking bilingual, bicultural workers who can interact well with international clients. Every cultural group has its own traditions, values, and business etiquette. Language barriers and lack of cultural sensitivity can lead to misunderstandings that can wreck business relationships. Bilingual, culturally diverse workers help businesses understand their international clients' perspectives, thereby improving business and customer relations and helping these businesses compete and grow internationally. As Ian Sells, the CEO and founder of RebateKey, a multimillion-dollar online business, makes clear, "Having multilingual workers can provide contextual information about people and places, which is beneficial in creating and establishing connections and relationships with business networks around the globe. Having multilingual employees also ensures that you understand another culture better, [bridge] gaps and ensure cultural sensitivity."[26]

Immigrants continue to play a key role in shaping and enriching American culture. In the process, they increase the nation's economic and social prosperity, creating cultural bonds that unite Americans with each other and with people all over the world.

CHAPTER FOUR

Shaping the Future

In 1992, sixteen-year-old Jan Koum and his mother were granted political asylum in the United States after fleeing anti-Semitism and social unrest in Soviet-controlled Ukraine. They settled in Mountain View, California. Even with the help of various agencies, life in America was not easy for the pair. They were very poor but managed to survive on the meager earnings Koum's mother made by babysitting and Koum earned sweeping the floor of a grocery store. Koum also attended high school. Although he did not own a computer, he learned computer programming in his spare time by studying computer manuals that he bought at a used bookstore. He was a fast learner, and his efforts paid off. His self-taught computer skills landed him a job at Yahoo.

During these early years, Koum tried to keep in touch with his friends and family in Ukraine, but it was challenging. Calling and texting abroad came with a high price tag. Moreover, as someone who had grown up in a nation that routinely listened in on and censored people's conversations, Koum distrusted the security of international calls and texts. Seeking a way to make long-distance communication affordable and secure, in 2009 Koum came up with an idea for a free messaging app. The app lets users send and receive calls and messages over the internet and protects the users' privacy with end-to-end encryption. He called it WhatsApp. As he explains,

A lot of what I experienced growing up in the USSR and coming to the US as an immigrant actually reflects itself in WhatsApp. Experiences from our youth shape what we do later in life. . . . I grew up in a country where I remember my parents not being able to have a conversation on the phone. The walls had ears, and you couldn't speak freely. Nobody should have the right to eavesdrop, or you become a totalitarian state—the kind of state I escaped as a kid.[27]

It took time, but the app eventually took off. Facebook (now Meta) purchased it in 2014 for $19.3 billion, making Koum and cofounder Brian Acton two of the richest men in the world. Since then, Koum has used his great wealth to help others prosper. In 2016, he established the Koum Family Foundation, a philanthropic organization that, so far, has donated approximately $1.5 billion to charitable causes throughout the world.

WhatsApp founders Brian Acton (left) and Jan Koum (right) are shown at the company headquarters in 2013. Koum, who emigrated from Ukraine as a teenager, came up with a way to make long-distance communication affordable and secure.

Through his hard work and social consciousness, Koum advanced the economy, made communication more secure, and enhanced many people's quality of life. As of 2023, an estimated 2 billion people worldwide used WhatsApp every month. It generates about $8.7 billion in annual revenue, mainly through its business application.

In his rise from rags to riches, Koum contributed greatly to his new homeland and to the world. He is just one of several extraordinary immigrants who achieved remarkable things and became extremely wealthy in the process. In fact, CNBC reports that more than half of the top tech companies in the United States were founded by immigrants or the children of immigrants.

Extraordinary People, Extraordinary Achievements

Pierre Omidyar, the creator of eBay, is another of these remarkable individuals. Like Koum, his interest in computer programming led him to develop a new web-based platform. It revolutionized e-commerce and, in the process, resulted in the creation of thousands of businesses and a new job sector. Omidyar was born in France in 1967 to Iranian parents who immigrated to France in pursuit of higher education. When Omidyar was six years old, the family relocated to Maryland, where Omidyar's father was employed as a physician and his mother accepted a position as a linguistics professor. Growing up, Omidyar was fascinated by business, commerce, and computer science. He designed his first computer program at age fourteen to help catalog the books in his middle school library.

Omidyar graduated from Tufts University in 1988 with a degree in computer science. At the time, the concept of web-based commerce was still developing. Omidyar was interested in its potential. So, in 1995, on a lark, he created a page on his personal website where visitors could sell and buy goods and services for auction. He called the page Auction Web. For fun, Omidyar listed a broken laser pointer on the page. He did not imagine anyone would bid on it, but to his surprise, it sold for $14.83.

As the days went by, more and more people visited the web page. It became so popular that Omidyar decided to build an entire website dedicated to online auctions, which he named eBay. The site exploded in popularity almost immediately. People were listing, selling, and buying everything imaginable. In response, Omidyar quit his day job working for a subsidiary of Apple to devote himself to eBay.

The business, which makes money by charging a small fee for each listing and a small percentage of final sales prices, quickly generated a profit. By the middle of 1997, it had become one of the most popular sites on the internet, hosting close to eight hundred thousand auctions per day. Not surprisingly, Omidyar became a billionaire when he took eBay public in 1998. And that was merely the beginning. From 1998 to 2022, the company's annual profits rose from $4 million to almost $10 billion. Even more importantly, Omidyar created a global online retail community that resulted in the creation of thousands of new businesses and a whole new job sector. As eBay spokesperson Amanda Pires points out, "An individual working alone can create a global business using eBay."[28]

The business is still growing. As of 2023, Omidyar was the 245th richest person in the world, according to *Forbes*. He and his wife, Pam, are part of a group of American billionaires who pledge to give away at least 50 percent of their massive wealth to help others. With this goal in mind, in 2004 the couple created the Omidyar Foundation, which is a philanthropic investment firm devoted to building a more equitable and inclusive society. Thus far, the foundation has committed $1.5 billion to organizations promoting social justice,

Sharing the Entrepreneurial Spirit

Chinedu Echeruo is an immigrant from Nigeria. He is also a tech expert, entrepreneur, and social activist. Echeruo was sixteen when his family came to the United States in 1989. Upon earning a master's degree in business administration from Harvard University, he took a job in investment banking in New York City. Echeruo often got lost navigating New York's complex public transportation system. Out of frustration, in 2005 he developed HopStop, a website and mobile app that helps people navigate public transportation systems in over six hundred cities throughout the world. He quit his job to run HopStop. It became so popular that Apple purchased it in 2013 for a large, undisclosed sum, making Echeruo a very rich man.

Echeruo also founded several other successful tech start-up companies. He has focused his attention on founding companies and developing technology that teaches others to become successful entrepreneurs. He believes that by empowering others to become entrepreneurs, he will help reduce poverty throughout the world, thereby making the world a better place for everyone.

including more than $100 million to charitable causes in Hawaii, where the Omidyars live. Through his efforts, Pierre Omidyar has already played a major role in shaping society and is expected to continue to make a significant impact in the years ahead.

Zooming Forward

Another immigrant, Eric Yuan, the creator of Zoom, is also shaping the future. When the world was locked down during the COVID-19 pandemic, people relied on Zoom to socialize, work, learn, and conduct business. The high-tech video communication platform revolutionized the way groups of people connect with each other via videoconferencing, webinars, and virtual meetings. Zoom is the brainchild of Yuan, a Chinese immigrant who earned two bachelor's degrees and a master's degree in China before coming to America in 1997.

While pursuing his master's degree, Yuan married his college sweetheart, Sherry. In fact, it was their relationship that sparked Yuan's interest in designing a video communication platform. Sherry lived more than ten hours away from Yuan by train. Due to the distance, the couple did not see each other as often as they would have liked. Yuan wanted to change this. He was determined to create a simple, inexpensive videoconferencing tool that would allow the couple to spend time together whenever they wanted. The technology to build such a platform was not yet available, but Yuan never gave up on his dream. He has always been persistent. In fact, after attending a conference in Japan where he heard Bill Gates speak, Yuan became determined to seek his fortune in Silicon Valley. His visa request, however, was denied eight times. A less persistent person might have given up. But Yuan kept reapplying until he was finally granted a visa in 1997. He recalls, "I realized the internet was going to change everything and that I had better embrace it as early as possible. I told my wife that I should figure out a way to get to the U.S. and join the first wave of the internet revolution. . . . After nine times trying to attain my visa, I got it. Looking back, it is more of a practice of my perseverance. . . . I did not give up."[29]

Upon relocating to Silicon Valley, Yuan was hired as a computer engineer by a start-up web conferencing company. The company was acquired by Cisco Systems in 2007, and Yuan was promoted to vice president of engineering. In this position, he was responsible for assisting clients who were having problems using the company's conferencing tools, which were difficult to use. Yuan thought he could design a better, simpler program. He approached Cisco with his idea, but the company was not interested in funding Yuan's project. So, in 2011, Yuan decided to strike out on his own. It took him two years to design and launch Zoom. It swiftly became a popular business communication tool. Yuan reached billionaire status when he took Zoom public in 2019.

An Essential Resource

Zoom's early success was just the start. When the COVID-19 pandemic struck, Zoom transitioned from serving as a business tool to becoming an essential resource for keeping society functioning. By April 2020, it had grown from 10 million daily meeting participants to 300 million. By allowing individuals working remotely to conduct business via virtual meetings, Zoom helped keep the economy going. Just as importantly, it became the chief way for people to connect socially. Using Zoom, groups held proms, family reunions, weddings, club meetings, and religious services, among numerous other get-togethers. And students all over the world attended classes via Zoom. In fact, to ensure that students throughout the world could continue their education during the shutdown, Yuan waived user fees for primary and secondary educational institutions.

After the pandemic ended, Zoom continued to grow. As of 2023, it reported having 6,787 employees and almost $4.4 billion in total annual revenues. Moreover, the platform (and others like it) changed the way people interact with each other and with technology. By enabling workers to easily collaborate with their colleagues around the globe virtually, Zoom changed the way people conduct business. As a result, hybrid working models have become more common. For his part, Yuan is working to refine Zoom so that it supports future flexible work models.

Yuan is also involved in supporting social causes. He, along with one thousand other wealthy Asian American business leaders, some of whom are immigrants too, vowed to jointly donate a total of $10 million to causes that combat racism and anti-Asian sentiment in the United States. "As a proud Asian American it is disheartening to see the hatred and violence against our community," Yuan said in a 2021 statement to CNBC. "Racism in any form is unacceptable and I feel strongly it is important to lend my voice and stand up with my colleagues, friends and family who are suffering during this time."[30]

The Mother of Emotion AI Technology

Egyptian American computer scientist Rana el Kaliouby is also determined to do the right thing for society. She is often called the mother of emotion AI (artificial intelligence) technology. Her groundbreaking work in developing AI software that detects and analyzes human emotions has already changed human lives and is expected to have an even greater impact in the future.

El Kaliouby grew up in Egypt. Upon earning a master's degree in computer science from the American University in Cairo in 2001, she attended Cambridge University in England. At Cambridge, she became interested in how computers can change the way people connect with each other and with technology and the role nonverbal communication plays in communication. She was especially intrigued with the idea of programming computers to recognize and measure human emotions through a person's vocal characteristics and facial expressions. These characteristics and expressions are known as vocal and facial biomarkers. As she explains,

Ninety percent of human communication is nonverbal—via our face, our voice, our body language and gestures. All that is lost online. It dawned on me that we have to redesign technology in a way that incorporates nonverbal communication. . . . There is evidence that facial and vocal biomarkers exist for things like depression, stress, anxiety or Parkinson's disease. While we're stuck with our devices for hours and hours every day, these could be opportunities to get a pulse on a person's mental and emotional state.[31]

By the time she completed her doctoral degree, she had created a program that could track several emotions. She called it MindReader. She also came up with the idea of constructing a wearable device that could help people with autism, who often struggle to recognize the meaning of facial expressions, monitor their own facial expressions. She theorized that by watching themselves, users would learn more about the relationship between facial expressions and emotion, which would help them improve their social skills.

The Children of Immigrants

The children of immigrants have contributed greatly to the United States. Steve Jobs, the creator of Apple, was the son of an immigrant, as was Ray Kroc, the owner of McDonald's, and animator and film producer Walt Disney. US senators Ted Cruz, Marco Rubio, and Tammy Duckworth, among other public servants, are also children of immigrants. The nation's first female, mixed-race vice president, Kamala Harris, and Colin Powell, its first Black secretary of state, are also children of immigrants.

Numerous studies reveal that the children of immigrants are an asset to American prosperity. A study by authors and economic professors Ran Abramitzky and Leah Boustan found that children of immigrants are good at moving up the economic ladder, no matter their parents' socioeconomic status or country of origin. They write, "The children of first-generation immigrants growing up close to the bottom of the income distribution . . . are more likely to reach the middle of income distribution than are children of similarly poor US-born parents." In fact, they are nearly twice as likely to become rich as the children of US-born parents who grew up with a comparable income level.

Ran Abramitzky and Leah Boustan, *Streets of Gold*. New York: Hatchette, 2022, p. 75.

While she was working on this device, she met Rosalind Picard, an MIT professor and a fellow pioneer in the field of emotion AI (also known as affective intelligence). Picard invited el Kaliouby to join her at MIT in 2005, which she did. Working together, the women built a wearable device that the *New York Times* included in its list of the top one hundred innovations of 2006. It consisted of a small camcorder that users hooked onto the side of glasses, and which was connected to a small computer. The camcorder recorded the wearer's face during a conversation, while the computer produced a graph that analyzed the wearer's facial expressions. By studying the video and the graph, individuals could better understand how to respond appropriately in social situations. "We used it to help individuals on the autism spectrum understand facial expressions, which a lot of them struggle with,"[32] el Kaliouby explained.

Developing More New Ideas

El Kaliouby envisioned emotion AI technology being used in other ways too. She foresaw it being used in vehicles to monitor driver inattention and drowsiness, by doctors to diagnose mood disorders like depression, and by businesses and advertisers to conduct market research, among other purposes. So, in 2009, she and Picard founded a new company named Affectiva with the goal of developing the appropriate software. As head of the company, el Kaliouby successfully created a multipurpose emotion recognition AI software that she called Affdex. Affdex serves as a tool kit for analyzing hundreds of facial expressions.

Interest in Affdex's many uses soared. Some prospective customers, however, wanted to use the program as a tool to spy on and manipulate the emotions of their employees and clients. El Kaliouby refused to allow her software to be used for that purpose despite the financial consequences. She is deeply concerned about the abuse of emotion recognition AI. In fact, she is a member of an international coalition of individuals and

Computer scientist Rana el Kaliouby is known for her groundbreaking work in developing face-scanning technology for detecting and analyzing human emotions. An Egyptian immigrant, her work has changed human lives.

organizations advocating for the responsible use of AI. "Technology," she maintains, "is moving really fast, and we need it right now. But that's no excuse to be sloppy. As we train young people to become the future AI leaders of the world, it's important that privacy and the unintended consequences of technology are part of the curriculum."[33]

Over the years, el Kaliouby has continued developing emotion AI software and advocating for its humane use. In 2019, Smart Eye, a Swedish AI company, purchased Affectiva for an estimated $72 million, and el Kaliouby was named Smart Eye's deputy CEO. The software she created is currently being used by one-quarter of all *Fortune* 500 companies as well as by people with developmental and cognitive challenges. El Kaliouby's work has made her a rich, influential woman, and she is dedicated to using her power for good. She serves on the boards of several organizations that are dedicated to increasing diversity and the role of women in computer science as well as ensuring that AI is used for public good. Her work is integral to the future of technology.

Indeed, the achievements of extraordinary immigrants like el Kaliouby, as well as the contributions of millions of other immigrants throughout history, helped make the United States a great and prosperous nation. In pursuit of the American dream, they brought about innovation, founded hugely successful businesses, encouraged the formation and growth of new industries, created jobs, and fostered economic growth and social prosperity. And, by continuing to advance the boundaries of what is possible, they are shaping the future.

Introduction: Immigrants Help Drive American Prosperity

1. Quoted in New American Economy, "Italian Immigrant Becomes Owner of Auto Body Shop in New Jersey," February 3, 2022. www.newamericaneconomy.org.
2. Quoted in *New Jersey Business Magazine*, "NJSBDC Network Honors Clients, Legislators and Media Members," December 8, 2014. www.njbmagazine.com.
3. Quoted in Peter Dizikes, "Study: Immigrants in the U.S. Are More Likely to Start Firms, Create Jobs," MIT News, May 9, 2022. www.news.mit.edu.
4. Quoted in Catherine E. Shoichet, "Undocumented Immigrants Are Paying Their Taxes Today, Too," CNN, April 18, 2023. www.cnn.com.
5. William J. Clinton, "Commencement Address at Portland State University in Portland, Oregon," American Presidency Project, June 13, 1998. www.presidency.ucsb.edu.

Chapter One: Hard Workers

6. Quoted in Michelle Andrews, "As Long-Term Care Staffing Crisis Worsens, Immigrants Can Bridge the Gaps," KFF Health News, February 3, 2023. www.kffhealthnews.org.
7. Quoted in Amine Rahal, *Immigrant Hustle*. Victoria, BC: Tellwell, 2020, pp. 63–64.
8. Quoted in Lauren Rosenblatt, "Finding Workers Was Already Hard for the Ag Industry. Now, It's Even Worse, Farmers Say," *USA Today*, July 3, 2021. www.usatoday.com.
9. Quoted in Ashish Malhotra, "Immigrant Doctors Fill US Healthcare Gaps—but Visa Rules Make Life Tough," *The Guardian*, June 2, 2021. www.theguardian.com.
10. Charles Elachi, "The Path to Mars Goes from Lebanon to Pasadena," What It Means to Be American, September 22, 2014. www.whatitmeanstobeamerican.org.
11. Quoted in Andrea Widener, "Science in the US Is Built on Immigration. Will They Keep Coming?," *Chemical & Engineering News*, March 4, 2019. https://cen.acs.org.

12. Quoted in New American Economy, "CEO Barry Zhang Says High Tech Manufacturing Companies Depend on Machine Operators from Abroad," September 13, 2016. www.newamericaneconomy .org.

13. Quoted in Paul Moses, "Irish-Americans: Remember from Whence You Came," CNN, March 16, 2017. www.cnn.com.

Chapter Two: Building and Connecting Communities

14. Quoted in Maya Rao, "How Did the Twin Cities Become a Hub for Somali Immigrants?," Minneapolis (MN) *Star Tribune,* June 21, 2019. www.startribune.com.

15. Quoted in Abdirizak Diis, "In Twin City Speech, Somali Prime Minister Praises Community, Asks for Support," MPR News, Minnesota Public Radio, September 25, 2023. www.mprnews.org.

16. Quoted in Ran Abramitzky and Leah Boustan, *Streets of Gold*. New York: Public Affairs, 2022, p. 121.

17. Quoted in Nelson J. Callihan and William F. Hickey, "Irish Americans of Cleveland," Cleveland Memory. www.clevelandmemory.org.

18. Quoted in Sherrie Wang, "A New American Dream: The Rise of Immigrants in Rural America," Civil Eats, March 22, 2019. www .civileats.com.

19. Quoted in CNN, "Schwarzenegger: No Country More Welcoming than the USA," August 31, 2004. www.cnn.com.

Chapter Three: Enriching American Culture

20. Quoted in Angeli Gabriel, "The History of St. Patrick's Day," Fox Weather, March 17, 2023. www.foxweather.com.

21. Lyndon B. Johnson, "Signing of the Immigration and Nationality Act," LBJ Presidential Library, October 3, 1965. www.lbjlibrary.org.

22. Quoted in Harmeet Kaur, "How Asian Americans Are Keeping Lunar New Year Traditions Alive," CNN, January 19, 2023. www.edition .cnn.com.

23. Quoted in Stephanie Serrano, "'Quinceañeras Move the Money Around Our Community,'" KUNR Public Radio, August 29, 2017. www.kunr.org.

24. Howard Reich, "How Immigrants Created America's Mix Tape," *Chicago Tribune*, July 12, 2013. www.chicagotribune.com.

25. Quoted in Kylie Ora Lobell, "Why Are Companies Hiring More Multilingual Workers?," Society for Human Resource Management, May 9, 2022. www.shrm.org.

26. Quoted in Lobell, "Why Are Companies Hiring More Multi-lingual Workers?"

Chapter Four: Shaping the Future

27. Quoted in David Shamah, "Immigrant Founder's Past a Major Part of WhatsApp's DNA," Times of Israel, February 20, 2014. www.timesofisrael.com.
28. Quoted in Leslie Taylor, "eBay Fuels Growth of Sole Proprietorships," *Inc.*, August 15, 2006. www.inc.com.
29. Quoted in Jason Nazar, "13 Leadership Lessons from Zoom Founder and CEO Eric Yuan," *Entrepreneur,* April 21, 2021. www.entrepreneur.com.
30. Quoted in Jennifer Liu, "Zoom CEO Eric Yuan and Hundreds of Asian American Business Leaders Pledge $10 Million to AAPI Causes," CNBC, April 1, 2021. www.cnbc.com.
31. Quoted in Steffan Heuer, "Why A-I Systems Should Become Emotionally Intelligent," Think:Act Magazine, January 11, 2021. www.rolandberger.com.
32. Quoted in K. Megan Lawrence, "How Entrepreneur & Tech CEO Rana el Kaliouby Learned to Pay It Forward," *Bustle,* August 13, 2020. www.bustle.com.
33. Quoted in Heuer, "Why A-I Systems Should Become Emotionally Intelligent."

Sources: Immigrant Contributions to American Prosperity (pages 4–5)

- Joel Rose, "The Immigrant Population in the U.S. Is Climbing Again, Setting a Record Last Year," NPR, September 14, 2023. www.npr.org.
- Shannon Schumacher, et al, "Understanding the U.S. Immigrant Experience: The 2023 KFF/LA Times Survey of Immigrants," Sep 17, 2023. www.kff.org.
- "Immigrants in the U.S. Economy: Overcoming Hurdles, Yet Still Facing Barriers," Immigration Research Initiative, May 1, 2023. https://immresearch.org.
- "New American Fortune 500 in 2023," American Immigration Council, August 29, 2023. www.americanimmigrationcouncil.org.
- "How Many Immigrants Are in the American Workforce?," USA Facts, November 14, 2023. https://usafacts.org.
- "Foreign-Born Workers: Labor Force Characteristics—2022," Bureau of Labor Statistics, May 18, 2023. www.bls.gov.
- "Immigrants in United States of America," American Immigration Council, 2024. https://map.americanimmigrationcouncil.org.
- "Immigrants in United States of America," American Immigration Council, 2024. https://map.americanimmigrationcouncil.org.

FOR FURTHER RESEARCH

Books

Jaqueline Backus, *A New History of Immigration.* New York: Penguin Workshop, 2022.

Eric Braun, *Immigrants Who Served the Nation.* Mankato, MN: Capstone, 2021.

George W. Bush, *Out of Many, One: Portraits of America's Immigrants.* New York: Crown, 2021.

Joann Mattern, *100 Immigrants Who Shaped American History.* Naperville, IL: Sourcebooks, 2023.

Ghazi Rayan, *Immigrants Who Founded and Fostered an Early Nation*. Charleston, SC: Palmetto, 2021.

Internet Sources

Sabri Ben-Achour and Alex Schroeder, "What Immigration Actually Does to Jobs, Wages and More," Marketplace Morning Report, December 12, 2023. https://www.marketplace.org.

Wendy Edelberg and David Dollar, "Why Immigrants Are America's Superpower," Brookings Institution, July 3, 2023. www.brookings.edu.

Vance Ginn, "Barriers to Immigration Are Barriers to Economic Prosperity for All," Library of Economics and Liberty, July 20, 2023. www.econlib.org.

Greg Rosalsky, "New Nation, New Ideas: A Study Finds Immigrants Out-Innovate Native-Born Americans," *Planet Money,* NPR, July 10, 2023. www.npr.org.

Tahmina Watson, "This July Fourth, Reflect on Immigrants' Contributions and Urge Reform," *Seattle Times,* July 3, 2023. www.seattletimes.com.

Websites

American Immigration Council

www.americanimmigrationcouncil.org

This is a Washington, DC–based nonprofit organization and advocacy group that strives for a fair and just immigration system. It provides information on many immigration-related topics, including "Economics of Immigration."

George W. Bush Presidential Center

www.bushcenter.org

The Bush Center is dedicated to advancing American democracy and prosperity. By searching for the word *immigration* on its website, users can access hundreds of articles about immigrants and immigration.

I Am an Immigrant

www.iamanimmigrant.com

This organization celebrates the contribution of immigrants to American communities. It features lots of personal stories written by immigrants on its website.

Immigrant Learning Center

www.ilctr.org

The Immigrant Learning Center is a nonprofit organization that supports immigrants and immigration. Visitors to its website can access statistics, research studies, reports on immigrant entrepreneurship and the economy, webinars, and a blog.

Migration Policy Institute (MPI)

www.migrationpolicy.org

The MPI is a nonpartisan organization that studies and analyzes immigration and immigration policies. It provides a wealth of information on every aspect of immigration on its website, including research studies, maps, and graphics.

New American Economy

www.newamericaneconomy.org

New American Economy is a nonprofit research organization that supports immigration policies that lead to economic growth. It provides lots of information about the contributions of immigrants, including statistics, graphics, research reports, and personal interviews on its website.